Selected Poems

LORNA GOODISON

Selected Poems

Ann Arbor

THE UNIVERSITY OF MICHIGAN PRESS

Published in the United States of America by
The University of Michigan Press
Manufactured in the United States of America
♾ Printed on acid-free paper

2002   2001   2000   1999   7   6   5   4

A CIP catalogue record for this book is available from the British Library.

Library of Congress Cataloging-in-Publication Data

Goodison, Lorna.
   [Poems. Selections]
   Selected poems / Lorna Goodison.
      p.   cm.
   ISBN 0-472-09493-9 (alk. paper). — ISBN 0-472-06493-2 (pbk. :
alk. paper)
      1. Caribbean Area—Poetry.   I. Title.
   PR9265.9.G6A6   1992
   811—dc20   92-31769
                                                    CIP

Grateful acknowledgment is made to New Beacon Press for permission to reprint the
following poems from Lorna Goodison's *I Am Becoming My Mother: My Last Poem;
Mulatta Song; Jamaica 1980; We Are the Women; Garden of the Women Once Fallen;
Dream—August 1979; Songs for My Son; My Will; Caravanserai; Mulatta Song II; The
Mulatta as Penelope; Farewell Our Trilogy; Tightrope Walker; Lepidopterist; On Becoming a
Mermaid; The Mulatta and the Minotaur; 'Mine, O Thou Lord of Life, Send My Roots
Rain'; Keith Jarrett—Rainmaker; Invoke Mercy Extraordinary for Angels Fallen; Lullaby
for Jean Rhys; I Am Becoming My Mother; Guinea Woman; For Rosa Parks; Bedspread;
Nanny: For My Mother;* and *Letters to the Egyptian;* and from the book *Heartease,* the
following poems: *I Shall Light a Candle; My Father Always Promised Me; A Forgiveness;
Songs of Release; My Last Poem (Again); She Walks into Rooms; Survivor; This is a Hymn;
Dream: Gleanings; Some Nights I Don't Sleep; Some of My Worst Wounds; Upon a Quarter
Million; In Anxiety Valley; Heartease I; Heartease II; Heartease III; Heartease New England
1987; Come Let Your Eyes Feel; Star Suite; The Pictures of My New Day; O Love You So
Fear the Dark; Farewell Wild Woman (I); Farewell Wild Woman (II); Ceremony for the
Banishment of the King of Swords; Blue Peace Incantation; And Your Being So Abundantly
Blessed with Names; A Rosary of Your Names;* and *Always Homing Now Soul Towards
Light.*

In memory of my father
Vivian Marcus Goodison
and to
Miles Goodison-Fearon

Contents

To Us, All Flowers Are Roses

Accompong is Ashanti, root, Nyamekopon
appropriate name Accompong, meaning
warrior or lone one. Accompong,
home to bushmasters, bushmasters being
maroons, maroons dwell in dense places
deep mountainous well sealed
strangers unwelcome. Me No Send You No Come.

I love so the names of this place
how they spring brilliant like "roses"
(to us all flowers are roses) engage you
in flirtation. What is their meaning? pronunciation?
a strong young breeze that just takes
these names like blossoms and waltzes
them around, turn and wheel them on the tongue.

There are angels in St. Catherine somewhere.
Arawak is a post office in St. Ann.
And if the Spaniards hear of this
will they come again in Caravelles
to a post office (in suits of mail)
to enquire after any remaining Arawaks?
Nice people, so gentle, peaceful, and hospitable.

There is everywhere here.
There is Alps and Lapland and Berlin.
Armagh, Carrick Fergus, Malvern
Rhine and Calabar, Askenish
where freed slaves went to claim
what was left of the Africa within,
staging secret woodland ceremonies.

Such ceremonies! such dancing, ai Kumina!
drum sound at Barking Lodge where we hear
a cargo of slaves landed free, because
somebody signed a paper even as they
rode as cargo shackled on the high seas.
So they landed here, were unchained, went free.
So in some places there is almost pure Africa.

Some of it is lost, though, swept away forever,
maybe at Lethe in Hanover, Lethe springs
from the Greek, a river which is the river
of Oblivion. There is Mount Peace here
and Tranquility and Content. May Pen
Dundee Pen, Bamboo Pen and for me,
Faith's Pen, therefore will I write.

There is Blackness here which is sugar land
and they say is named for the ebony of the soil.
At a wedding there once the groom wore cobalt blue
and young bride, cloud white, at Blackness.
But there is blood, red blood in the fields
of our lives, blood the bright banner flowing
over the order of cane and our history.

The Hope River in hot times goes under
but pulses underground strong enough to rise
again and swell to new deep, when the May rains
fall for certain. There was a surfeit once
of Swine in Fat Hog quarter and somehow
Chateau Vert slipped on the Twi of our tongue
and fell to rise up again as "Shotover."

They hung Paul Bogle's body at sea
so there is blood too in the sea, especially
at Bloody Bay where they punctured balloons
of great grey whales. There is Egypt here
at Catadupa, a name they spoke first softly

2

to the white falling cataracts of the Nile.
There is Amity and Friendship and Harmony Hall.

Stonehenge, . . . Sevens, Duppy Gate, Wait a Bit,
Wild Horses, Tan and See, Time and Patience,
Unity. It is Holy here, Mount Moses
dew falls upon Mount Nebo, south of Jordan,
Mount Nebo, rises here too hola Mount Zion high.
Paradise is found here, from Pisgah we look out
and Wait a Bit Wild Horses, Tan and See Time and Patience.

Unity, for the wounded a Doctor's Cave
and at Phoenix Park from Burnt Ground new rising.
Good Hope, the mornings dawn crystalline
at Cape Clear. It is good for brethren
and sistren to dwell together in Unity
on Mount Pleasant. Doctor Breezes issue from the side
of the sea across parishes named for saints.

Rivers can be tied together in eights.
Mountains are Lapis Lazuli or Sapphire
impossibly blue and rivers wag their waters
or flow Black or White or of Milk.
And the waters of the Fish River do contain
and will yield up good eating fish. O heart
when some night you cannot sleep

for wondering why you have been charged
to keep some things of which you cannot speak,
think what release will mean, when your name
is changed to Tranquility. I was born at Lineen—
Jubilee!—on the anniversary of Emancipation Day.
I recite these names in a rosary, speak them
when I pray, for Heartease, my Mecca, aye Jamaica.

New York Is a Subway Stop—1969

It may lose its song
in this final translation,
for I have written it
many times before, running
without subway stop
through my mind.
But facing the wall
my neighbor who speaks
through street cries
I write it down as it unfolds.

All the things New York is.
Like the sight of odd lovers
Odd couples, the film that
forever runs at Radio City
forever odd as the infallible
routine of the Rockettes.
Lovers who kiss at busy
intersections or the hard-
to-distinguish lovers in Greenwich
Village where it is always
Christmas.

This girl and her guy who
love over steaming
cups of coffee, she with
awning-like lashes and
many fingers wearing
many rococo rings,
brushing strands of rain-brown
hair from her face as she

tells him again and again
that his friends are like
nowhere.
The love New York seems to
have invented and patented
and everyone is Honey and
American sweet.

New York is the boy from Jamaica
you recognize, because he's
asleep in the subway, probably
has two jobs. And the girl you
know who left home for here
ten years ago, and she has the
same face, only it's not her
but a Spanish girl who speaks
no English but smiles gold-
toothedly.

New York is the most beautiful
boy I have ever seen, standing
lyrical against the door of the
train. Hair Negro naturally
and tribal dress to hips
meeting his western pants
and loafers.
The most beautiful boy whose
hands grow from the sleeves
of his African blouse and
clutch a Baldwin book.
This boy and his natural
girl and the fine line of his
profile and you smile because
people are beautiful.
New York is the rush of subways
and the birth of commuters into
humid summer streets.

A Chinese family from the Ming
Dynasty, four pairs of tiny feet
and alabaster faces.

New York is the big truck driver
who grins and says "curly
head Nigger you're beautiful."
New York is the silent oath
taken by the people who
clutch the iron pole hand clasp
above hand clasp "I swear
to ride the IRT forever."
New York is Graffiti
"Whitey got to go, Paint
the White House black,"
or simply "lots of good luck."

New York is the dental work of
the Brooklyn Bridge and the
incongruous rocks in Central
Park. The navy blue grimace
of policemen and the eternal
rush-splendor of Fifth Avenue.
It is "the Ultimate Painting" safe
inside the Museum of Modern
Art, and you wonder at these cats
and how right they are, for the
ultimate painting is completely
black.

New York is the clean hippie who
looks like Christ is supposed
to have looked and Black is
Beauty.
New York is my subway
stop. Fulton, Sterling,

Winthrop.
Funny name Flatbush.

My stop, Church,
proclaimed in mosaic
Wait for the walk light
Fumble for your keys
And the stain on the top
step announces
my flight.
New York is love
and lonely
and what I've seen,
"Go upstate"
there are three trees
growing in this Brooklyn
Yard.
"Sock it to me summer."

Sister Mary and the Devil

I was going down the road
and the two o'clock sun
only beating down on the
roses on Brother Williams wreath
till them curl up like them want to
sleep,
and is only me and God
alone
going down the road.

the dust was powdering
mi clean white shoes
when I look down
and see me shadow double.

I know him was the devil,
him never have to tell me
because mi blood start to run
and stop
and heavy down mi step
and the ground leave
mi foot
and mi heart like it want
stop
and I wash wid cold sweat.

The devil himself
a tall man in full black
with a hat that cover him
face like a umbrella.
Then him take Brother Williams

wreath from me
and him hold mi round mi waist
and fire catch in mi body
and I shame and hide mi face,
and then him talk for the first
time,
and it was there
Sister Mary died
when the devil
in him
satan voice
hold on to
the wreath and said
today is mine Sister Mary
let the dead
bury the dead.

Letter to My Love

My love,
cloven hooves
separate our steps
deflect our signals
through distance.

Since last I saw you
the goat boy played
his last note.
It fell somewhere

in the rain forest
and bloomed!

No, not a shepherd's bush

but flesh-petaled flowers
with the fragrance of aloes
but in such colors!

The forest (as you know)
is not far from my window
the wind brought me some seeds
dropped on the slopes of me
ploughed by you so well

I bloomed.

Since then,

mere men fear me.

When picked,

I shriek, bleed, ache,

someone I have heard

has called me a Mandrake

Yet others say . . .

But the sea

is not our territory.

I wait without your forest.

Guyana Lovesong

I, torn from the center of
some ladies' novel
drift a page across strange
landscape.

Resting on open-faced lily pads,
melting in slow rain canals,
sliding by sentinel grass in
a savanna,
I crossed the mighty Rupununi
River,
returned limp on the bow of
a ferry.
Timheri.
The way to calm in your eyes.
The river without guile in your
eyes.

Wash over the edges of your woman's
sorrow.

Time is one continent till tomorrow.

On Houses

I have built many houses
made warm smells in as many kitchens
created content within
according to the color of the season.

The first were by definition rooms,
with corners I squared into other rooms.
Encouraged by this success,
the time for the season approached me.

You later led me to believe
I led you to the house
of seasonal white
down the garden deep with dreams.

But the kitchen grew electric
spun me away from it.
When you were not looking
flung me against the dowry chest,
I went upstairs to rest.

To lie in the bedroom adrift
with white curtains blowing you
good-bye as you went to sea
in a boat lined with careful money.
Yet that house was not the last,
you commissioned one of newest glass,
I tinkled,
and tried to create calm smells
in that transparent kitchen.
You fenced it in when I was not looking.

13

I finger chains and make clinking noises
in key.
And watch the garden grow reproaches.

I'm inclined to think I'll build no more houses.

The Road of the Dread

That dey road no pave
like any other black-face road
it no have no definite color
and it fence two side
with live barbwire.

And no look fi no milepost
fi measure you walking
and no tek no stone as
dead or familiar

for sometime you pass a ting
you know as . . . call it stone again
and is a snake ready fi squeeze yu
kill yu
or is a dead man tek him
possessions tease yu.
Then the place dem yu feel
is resting place because time
before that yu welcome like rain,
go dey again?
bad dawg, bad face tun fi drive yu underground
wey yu no have no light fi walk
and yu find sey that many yu meet who sey
them understand
is only from dem mout dem talk.
One good ting though, that same treatment
mek yu walk untold distance
for to continue yu have fe walk far
away from the wicked.

Pan dis same road ya sista
sometime yu drink yu salt sweat fi water
for yu sure sey at least dat no pisen,
and bread? yu picture it and chew it accordingly
and some time yu surprise fi know how dat full
man belly.

Some day no have no definite color
no beginning and no ending, it just name day
or night as how you feel fi call it.

Den why I tread it brother?
well mek I tell yu bout the day dem
when the father send some little bird
that swallow flute fi trill me
and when him instruct the sun fi smile pan me first.

And the sky calm like sea when it sleep
and a breeze like a laugh follow mi.
Or the man find a stream that pure like baby mind
and the water ease down yu throat
and quiet yu inside.

And better still when yu meet another traveler
who have flour and yu have water and man and man
make bread together.
And dem time dey the road run straight and sure
like a young horse that cant tire
and yu catch a glimpse of the end
through the water in yu eye
I wont tell yu what I spy
but is fi dat alone I tread this road.

Wedding in Hanover

The elected virgins
bathe together

gather by the traditional
river
the same water
that calmed my mother
on the morning they gave her
to my father

Roseapple scented
is the bridal path,
is the amniotic color
and the mountains
lock our purdah

The bride is nubile
bless her
small high belly,
may it rise
and multiply
multiply

Later,
dressed in shades of
bougainvillea
newly cleansed by
the family river,
the elected virgins
attend her, and
the bride is virgin
as the river.

Bridge Views

The railings along the gully bridge
were really diviners' signs.
Parallel, they spelt equal,
in reality they pointed west
to the future.
Sites Rema, Jungle, and the esoterica
of Tivoli.
The boys on the gully bridge
Rufus, George, Donkey Knee, and
Curriman. My brothers numbering
five, till the little one

grew big enough to represent the half-
dozen Goodison men on the bridge.

There was the night the masked Indian
transporting the night soil of his
terrible occupation
angered by the cries of "ah know yu?"
turned and flicked his whip.
And the tip marked like snake spit
the red face of Curriman.

In the land of little boy loyalty
their friend became "shit whip."

Knowing no class lines or shoes
they roamed through fields
of police macca.

Played bat-up-and-ketch
and watched Gussie and Lloyd
wrestle with the early locks of
Rasta.

My mother did not forget to tell us
we did not really belong there.
Her family gave their name to rivers
her children should not play in gullies
we were always on our way back to where
she, originally petite bourgeoisie, came from,

so we moved.

Up the road past One Son
who never played by the bridge
but hurried by, his fat thighs
rubbing together clutching
his errands evidence.
Shillin ice.

We moved to concrete suburbia
acquiring the first weapon for
committing class suicide.
At first the boys would come
to the phenomenon of this house

near the sea with a beach

and proper boundaries.
Unlike the schizoid waters
of the Hunts Bay Power Station
the heated pool of Kingston's poor
children.

And they came.

till Georgie tief some electric wire
from the hardware store
and Mike discovered the healing in white rum
till all his teeth fell out
to make way for more rum
and the neighborhood was providing
addresses for murder cases.
And One Son shed his fat
and made the front page
of the Star
as the paid stepper of a
political figure
and more than that he broke out
of penitentiary
and shot a guard as he hurried past.

The railings on the bridge
parallel spell equal still
and what is now curfew zone
was then just Home.

For the Tall Comrade

You came, taller than the frame of my door
your shadow peaked behind you.

You stood, taller than the shadow of that door

pausing only to nod your arriving.

And the presence lifted the frame of that door
higher for your entrance.
And having come
you stayed.

"And what will you do to hold my attention?"
"As you may have heard, I'm fond of flight."

"I have come prepared," you answer.
Your fingers ease a shadow from the corner
of my eye.

Keen as blades, shave it into a shape
"here, a baby bird."
You breathe through a nutmeg, life.
settle it among my breasts.

You do not speak much, but I have learnt
that that is your way.

But each day I find a new shape
resting on a pillow

blooming from a clay pot
growing in my belly.
Sometimes you color them topaz
so I say, "it's your eyes"
and you say, "no it's the sun."

The balance of my house's chiaroscuro
is becoming uneven
"why have you cut up all my shadows?"
"watch this one"
and the blades fly again.

From your fingers grow
Africa.

"But how can you give me Africa?"

"simple," you say, breaking your continent
of silence.

We'll build the house of terra-cotta.
Our images will imitate Benin
and the child will know about Soweto

and the trees will have West African roots

and the shape of the silence settles.

Tonight the Limpopo is running under
the window

and the shape of tomorrow's shadow
is spreading between your fingers
like revolution.

Judges

"Unhappiness is not grounds for divorce."

"Marriage does not guarantee happiness."

"This court does not support women's liberation."

Well hear this! Those are my grounds as a poet!

This court does not support women's liberation.

Therefore, sir, you do not recognize the daughters
of the revolution.

You with the poodlewig and Johncrow covers about you,
recognize them!
They are working in your kitchen
cooking compliments for your slow-witted wife.

They are used to biting their lips under the
violation of your sons
for whose first experience you chose a young
clean maid.

You do not recognize Imogene and Joyce and Irma?
The daughters of the Loyal Levi and the Auxiliary?
They who sprout white wings on Sundays
their bosoms breathing orchid powder?

They support themselves like me.

Some have surpassed the strength of men.
Imogene has the strength of ten,
She has sent gunmen into bowed retreat.
And Irma who raise the red flag like Mother-Banna
Suck more bullet for the party than any man.

And you do not recognize women's liberation?

Do you know the infinity of my mother's strength?
Do you know the resilience of my epileptic sister?
My grandmother fell from the height of her horse

at age one hundred and one
and you do not recognize women's liberation?

And nobody told you I was a poet?
You who sit in judgment on the ones who come
moved by the nongrounds of unhappiness?
I am lining up these words
holding them behind the barrier of my teeth

biding my time as only a woman can.

I have a poem for you, judge man.

Kenscoff

In Kenscoff Market the breeze brought spices
and Michelle sells broad-leaf mint, tibom.
And what do you sell Marcel?

Arum lilies pouting for deep rain kisses
and gladioli in colors of berries.
Would I had enough soap bars
the color of creole
for I sell soap bars

and I have built mansions of soap bars
and the wind whistles through my architecture.

My brother is chained in the iron market
he is a hacking artist of tourist keepsakes.
The others work on stone by moonlight,
they move gypsum mountains by hand,

some of us eat stone.

In Kenscoff market the breeze brought spices,
we pay for them with rain.

And a legend that Toussaint rides still.
Proof, the sobbing you hear is not the wind

it's him.

Gordon Town Morning

Gordon Town this morning
was the dalliance of Ralph Campbell
in slack flirtation with a fat cloud.
She's lifted her dress
and is wheeling her cumulous frocktail
over the heads of the church and courthouse
spires.

The wheels direct themselves
over the wedge of that same bridge
where Nigel my brother
and I his fat dreaming sister
would wait for our morning drive.
"Morning Children" . . . "Morning sir"
                    . . . "Morning sir."
The silence changing gears, till
"Goodbye Children" . . . "Goodbye sir"
                    . . . "Goodbye sir."

The first poetry then of gold-filigree Poui
I longed to live at Mill-in-Spring
a displaced heroine with a faceless lover.

Years later throughout the same streets a frightened bride.
Now a woman with a face that has earned every line.
It was nothing my springtime, it was nothing my smile.
She loved a young warrior. Her brother took a bride.
It was nothing my brother/compañero/it happened before.
And Wai Rua does not lead to home anymore.

26

Tamarind Season

The skin atrophies
to a case of spinster brown.

The soft welcome within
needs protecting
so she grows wasp-waisted.
again
wasp-waisted

The welcome turns sour
she finds a woman's tongue
and clacks curses at the wind
for taking advantage

box her about this way
and that is the reason

wait is the reason

Tamarind Season.

Whose Is That Woman?

Who is that woman?

Hair streaked by shooting stars (near misses)

her smile's a wet moonstone at morning.

Who is the woman?

Her skirt's motion stirs, sandalwood rises

the pads of her feet, pear-shaped, walk softer.

Who is this woman?

Her heart encased in virgin tissue,
be careful how you know her.

Whose is that woman?

Her house walls mixed
with some sea-salt solution/tears/salt-water.

Who is that woman?

She is fragile, there is an egg within her.

In her bosom it's always flow-time,

her body melts at morning

you may drink her.

28

For Don Drummond

Dem say him born
with a caul,
a not-quite-opaque
white veil
through which he visioned
only he knew.

At birth dem suppose
to bury it
under some special tree.
If we had known
we could have told them
it was to be,
the Angel Trombone Tree.

Taptadaptadaptadada . . .
Far far East
past Wareika
down by Bournemouth
by the sea,
the Angel Trombone
bell-mouthed sighs
and notes like petals rise
covering all a we.

Not enough notes
to blow back the caul
that descend regularly
and cover this world vision
hiding him from we.

Find a woman
with hair like rivers,
a waist unhinged
and free;
emptied some of the sorrow
from the horn's cup;
into the well below her belly.

She promised to take the caul
from his eyes:
to remove the cold matter
that clouded his eyes;
and stand between him
and
the trombone tree duppy.
The promise dead like history.
Dead like she.

When the caul come again
and covered his eyes,
this time the blade rise
like notes in a scandal
on a street corner
Far far East
past Wareika.

From a Bridge view
the crowd holds notes
One gone . . .
Don gone . . .

Lay me down for the band must rest / Yes, Music
    is my occupation
I tired a hold this note / you hold this memory
    For J.F.K., For Me
Mek the slide kotch / is right here so I stop

Belleview is the view I view / Sometime I think
   the whole world mad too.

Behold the house of his feet,
the brown booga
tongue ajar, a door that blow and open and close
   no more.

Fold the dark suit pressed under newspaper,
"Murder" screamed the morning paper,
bring the felt hat
where the caul would hide
to slip down sly and cover his eyes.

And this time do the burial right fi we
Bury the Don under the Angel Trombone Tree.

My Last Poem

I once wrote poems
that emerged so fine
with a rough edge for honing
a soft cloth for polishing
and a houseproud eye
I'd pride myself in making them shine.
But in this false winter
with the real cold to come
no, this season's shift
there are no winters here,
well call it what you will but the cold time is here
with its memorial crosses to mark
my father's dying
and me wondering where next year will find me
in whose vineyard toiling.
I gave my son
to a kind woman to keep
and walked down through the valley
on my scarred feet,
across the river
and into the guilty town
in search of bread
but they had closed the bakery down.
So I returned and said child
there was no bread
I'll write you my last poem instead.
My last poem is not my best
all things weaken towards the end.
O but it should be laid out
and chronicled, crazy like my life
with a place for all my several lives

daughter, sister, mistress, friend, warrior
wife
and a high holy ending for the blessed
one
me as mother to a man.
There should be a place for
messages and replies
you are too tightly bound, too whole
he said
I loosened my hair and I bled
now you send conflicting signals they said
divided I turned both ways and fled.
There should be a place for all this
but I'm almost at the end of my last poem
and I'm almost a full woman.
I warm my son's clothes
in this cold time
in the deep of my bosom
and I'm not afraid of love.
In fact, should it be
that these are false signals I'm receiving
and not a real unqualified ending
I'm going to keep the word love
and use it in my next poem.
I know it's just the wordsmith's failing
to forge a new metal to ring like its rhyme
but I'll keep its fool's gold
for you see it's always bought me time.
And if I write another poem
I'm going to use it
for it has always used me
and if I ever write another poem
I'm going to return that courtesy.

We Are the Women

We are the women
with thread bags
anchored deep in our bosoms
containing blood agreements
silver coins and cloves of garlic
and an apocrypha
of Nanny's secrets.

We've made peace
with want
if it doesn't kill us
we'll live with it.

We ignore promises
of plenty
we know that old sankey.

We are the ones
who are always waiting
mouth corner white
by sepulchers and
boneyards
for the bodies of our men,
waiting under massa
waiting under massa table
for the trickle down of crumbs.

We are the women
who ban our bellies
with strips from the full moon
our nerves made keen

from hard grieving
worn thin like
silver sixpences.

We've buried our hope
too long
as the anchor to our
navel strings
we are rooting at
the burying spot
we are uncovering
our hope.

Mulatta Song

Very well Mulatta,
this dance must end.
This half-arsed band
blowing its own
self-centered song.
The bass slack stringed
slapped by some wall-eyed
mother's son.
This session must done
soon done.
O how you danced Mulatta
to the music in your head
pretending that their notes
were your notes.
Till the gateman whispered
into the side of your head
"Mulatta, mulatta, that's the
dance of the dead."
So you rubadub and rentatile
and hustle a little
smiling the while
pretending that
this terrible din
is a well-tuned air
on a mandolin.
And Mulatta your red dress
you wore here as new
is a wet hibiscus
what will you do?
Fold the petals of the skirt
and sit this last long

last song out.
Bind up the blood-wound
from the heart on your sleeve.
And now Mulatta it's time to leave.

Jamaica 1980

It trails always behind me
a webbed seine with a catch of fantasy
a penance I pay for being me
who took the order of poetry.
Always there with the gaping holes
and the mended ones, and the stand-in words.
But this time my Jamaica
my green-clad muse
this time your callings are of no use
I am spied on by your mountains
wire-tapped by your secret streams
your trees dripping blood-leaves
and jasmine selling tourist-dreams.

For over all this edenism
hangs the smell of necromancy
and each man eats his brother's flesh
Lord, so much of the cannibal left
in the jungle on my people's tongues.

We've sacrificed babies
and burnt our mothers
as payment to some viridian-eyed God dread
who works in cocaine under hungry men's heads.

And mine the task of writing it down
as I ride in shame round this blood-stained town.
And when the poem refuses to believe
and slimes to aloes in my hands
mine is the task of burying the dead
I the late madonna of barren lands.

Garden of the Women Once Fallen

I

SHAME MI LADY

Lady, what could you have done so
to make you close in on yourself so?

The lady folds her arms across her chest
The lady droops her head between her breasts.

The lady's eyes will not answer yours.
Lady, if I tell you my crime
will you tell me yours?

Mine are legion and all to do with love misplaced
yet I've been replanted in this arboreal place,
now, if I can find favor (me with my bold face)
you bashful you shy you innocent lady
must/bound to find absolution/grace.

Come lady, tie bright ribbon-grass round your waist
Let you and I bloom redemption in this place.

II

BROOM WEED

You exhaust yourself so
O weed powerless
your life devoted to sweeping, cleaning
even in your fullest blooming.
You pull dust balls from the air
whisk away bee-droppings

39

with your coarsened hair.
And in your fullness
they bundle you
without so much
as a by-your-leave.
Drudges, make a coat of arms
wear broomweed on your sleeves.

III

POUI

She don't put out for just anyone.
She waits for HIM
and in his high august heat
he takes her
and their celestial mating
is so intense
that for weeks her rose-gold dress
lies tangled round her feet
and she don't even notice.

IV

SUNFLOWER POSSESSED

Her folded neck-skin
reveals her age
but the face powdered
is limned by myriads
of mirrors and gold-washed frills.
This display is for the benefit
of the perfect one in the sky.
To the ragged coterie of weeds round her
she says, "In my first bloom I was
the tender honey-skinned mamma
of that great golden one on high."
The ragged weeds
never knowing glory

(for this reason some weeds are evil)
shiver their rags and hiss
"sure"
she semaphores, hoping
the golden circle of her unmaking
will give her the go-round once more.

Dream—August 1979

The sacrificial pigeon clears the roof.
The sun strikes,
his heart sprouts a hibiscus
glowing primary red
he too has joined the feathered ranks of the dead.
On Mount Zion the obeah man balms
on the battlefield below we with
bloodied hands
sight-read psalms.
The deed is done, the chosen have won.
And over Mount Rosser a wash-line flags
squares in bird's-eye say there is a babe within.
Only the bush promises healing.

Songs for My Son

I

My son cries
the cats answer
I hover over his sleeping
suspended on his milk-stained breath
I live in fear of his hurt, his death.
The fear is real
if I close my eyes when it is at its height
I see him curled man-in-miniature asleep.
I hover over his milk-stained breath
and listen for its rise
every one an assurance that he is alive
and if God bargains
I strike a deal with him,
for his life I owe you something, anything,
but please let no harm come to him.
The cat cries
my son answers
his sleep is short
his stomach hurts.

II

They gather from beyond
through the trees they come
gather on the banks of the family river
one by one they raise the keening song
great grandmother Rebecca of the healing hands
Tata Edward, Bucky, and Brownman
my father's lost mother Maria
and now my father

come to sing the birthsong
and Hannah horsewoman to ride me through.
It's a son, a great grand grandson, a man
born to a headstrong, heartfoolish woman,
part the birth waters with river-washed hands
and let the newson through,
woman born of strong-limbed woman
woman born to parents in peacetime
behold your son
flesh of your flesh
your life's work begun.

III

The midwife
tie-head African woman
fingers like healing-roots
feeds me thyme-tea
to hurry on your coming
summons the appropriate spirits
to witness your crowning,
a knife keen with garlic
to sever you from me
and we'll never smell
its primal top-notes
you or I
without memories of our joining.

IV

I'll name you Miles I say
for the music, and for coming
a long way
you suck, my womb pulls
the thirst constant
the connection three-way.

My Will

Son, my will,
albeit premature
when the palm readers
divine
for me an extended
life line.

Besides who knows what
worth bequeathing
I could acquire
before the life line
inches to the darker side
of my hand.

But, for a start,
the gift of song,
this sweet immediate source
of release was not given me
so I leave it for you in the hope
that God takes hints.
Then the right to call
all older than you
Miss, mister, or mistress
in the layered love of our
simplest ways,
eat each day's salt and bread
with praise,
and may you never know hungry.
And books
I mean the love of them.

May you like me earn good
friends
but just to be sure,
love books.
When bindings fall apart
they can be fixed
you will find
that is not always so
with friendships.
And no gold.
Too many die/kill for it
besides its face is too bold.
This observation is the
last I give:
most times assume a
patina a shade subdued
so when you bloom they
will value it.   .

Caravanserai

Elliptical moon
rims the yellow/brown
woman
dream seller.
Brass basins of blood
brass basins of wine
a pebbled hourglass
to texture time.

She dyes her palms
and divines on sand.
The moon bellied-out
stirs the tides' motion
within
the infant heads down
for the beginning.
The tide water breaks
the motion stays her hand.

And did you see
that quiet caravan
with muffled bells
and no colors to speak of
except the face
ebony/indigo
of the young camel driver
dream buyer?

He spoke to her of nights
by the Nile,
said there was Egypt

in her hair
and watered down
at the caravanserai there.

The woman
bends to deliver
by a tributary
of the Euphrates river
where lions drink
and an occasional hyena.
Brass basins of blood
brass basins of water.

Mulatta Song II

Mulatta of the loose-sieved hands
frail madonna of blood-stained lands

Yes I am the lady
this is the right door
the house covered in green
the red lantern
the grey and white cats
and the secrets
in the sandalwood box.
You've come seeking
a poem you say
and somebody directed you
this way?
Yes this is the house
of the lady poet
she wears black and heavy silver
there is calm within
when evening comes
she offers you wine
and sometimes her smile
and sometimes herself
but mostly she sits
and sings to herself.

The Mulatta as Penelope

Tonight I'll pull your limbs through small
soft garments
your head will part my breasts
and you will hear a different heartbeat.
Today we said the real good-bye, he and I
but this time
I will not sit and spin and spin
the door open to let the madness in
till the sailor finally weary
of the sea
returns with tin souvenirs and a claim
to me.
True, I returned from the quayside
my eyes full of sand
and his salt leaving smell
fresh on my hands.
But you're my anchor awhile now
and that goes deep,
I'll sit in the sun and dry my hair
while you sleep.

Farewell Our Trilogy

No, love, there are no new poems
not since the monsoon of six months or so.
Once or twice I've felt what I thought
was water breaking three days running
but it turned out to be playbacks from
your leaving. The only news
is that sometime on Sunday
a boy from the village above here
said he saw Sheba-cat in the dry-river bed
her throat stained, her long legs stiffened
in death, and, yes, as always
she had been quick with kittens.
But she's laid her down on the cool river stones
and exchanged her ninth life for
peace deep to the bones
and I'm writing this finally to say
that our cat was the last proof
that you and I mated
and raised up houses with the pillars
of our great love that corroded into hatred
and on Monday it rained hard
enough to bear her out to sea.
In this place I'm all that remains
of our trilogy.

Tightrope Walker

And I have been a tightrope walker all my life,
that is, tightrope walking has been my main occupation.
In between stints in sundry fraudulent circuses
I've worked at poetry, making pictures,
or being a paid smart-arse.
Once I even tried my hand at cashiering,
couldn't balance the ledger though
but I was honest, always overpaid someone
and I had to make up the shortfall myself.
But it was too firm on the ground
so I put on my fishnet tights
my iridescent kingfisher blue bathing suit
chalked the soles of my slippers of pliable gold kid
and took to the ropes again.

It's a fine life, those uncontained moments
in the air
those nerve-stretched belly-bottom spasms
from here to there
and your receiver copping what
from the ground looks like
an innocent feel
as he steadies you safely on the far side.
But I broke both arms
and the side of my head once
and had multiple miscarriages from
falling flat on my back
so I'm on the ground most days now
except for this, the tightest walk of all.
I don my new costume of
marabou and flamingo feathers

and my shade-of-oyster juliet cap
with the discreet spangles
and inch toward you once or twice a week.
I have to make record time
you have to be home before dark
and the entire act is really a rehearsal
here in this empty tent with last night's
sawdust to buffer the wild in our talk
and the fat lady sunning herself outside
and listening for secrets in our laughter
and it's all done with safety nets, thank you
and no audience invited to the finest
performances of me and you
but it's my life and my last act
before our show closes down
and reopens to a gaping public
at some other circus ground.

Lepidopterist

I've done my best to immortalise what I failed to keep.
　　　　　　　　　　—Joseph Brodsky

And now I am a lepidopterist
with my rows of bitter pins
securing here, now there
the flown species wings.
If we soak the memories
in our bile
they will keep and crystallize
come clear
in the heat of this now poisoned air.
I thought I had you / where are you?
You gave up on us / I gave up on you
You changed your mind / I'm changing mine
Lord, even in death the wings beat so.
Hold still
let me put this last row in.

On Becoming a Mermaid

Watching the underlife idle by
you think drowning must be easy death
just let go and let the water carry you
away and under
the current pulls your bathing-plaits loose
your hair floats out straightened by the water
your legs close together fuse all the length down
your feet now one broad foot
the toes spread into
a fish-tail, fan-like,
your sex locked under
mother-of-pearl scales
you're a nixie now, a mermaid
a green-tinged fish/fleshed woman/thing
who swims with thrashing movements
and stands upended on the sea floor
breasts full and floating buoyed by the salt
and the space between your arms now always
filled and your sex sealed forever under
mother-of-pearl scale/locks closes finally
on itself like some close-mouthed oyster.

"Mine, O Thou Lord of Life, Send My Roots Rain"

—Gerard Manley Hopkins

For I've been planted long
in a sere dry place
watered only occasionally
with odd overflows
from a passing cloud's face.
In my morning
I imitated the bougainvillea
(in appearances
I'm hybrid)
I gave forth defiant alleluias
of flowering
covered my aridity with
red-petaled blisters
grouped close, from far
they were a borealis of
save-face flowers.
In the middle of my
life span
my trunk's not so limber
and sap flows thicker
my region has posted signs
that speak of scarce water.
At night God, I feel
my feet powder.
Lord let the preying worms
wait to feast in vain.
In this noon of my orchard
send me deep rain.

Keith Jarrett—Rainmaker

Piano man
my roots are african
I dwell in the center of the sun.
I am used to its warmth
I am used to its heat
I am seared by its vengeance
(it has a vengeful streak)

So my prayers are usually
for rain.
My people are farmers
and artists
and sometimes the lines
blur
so a painting becomes a
december of sorrel
a carving heaps like a yam hill
or a song of redemption wings
like the petals of resurrection
lilies—all these require rain.
So this sunday
when my walk misses
my son's balance on my hips
I'll be alright if you pull down
for me
waterfalls of rain.
I never thought a piano
could divine
but I'm hearing you this morning
and right on time
its drizzling now

I'll open the curtains and
watch the lightning conduct
your hands.

Invoke Mercy Extraordinary for Angels Fallen

In his 30th year
in search of signs
God's face appeared to him
on the surface of a brackish pond
littered with leaves.
The face of God
was so suffused with light
light so intense
that the rotting leaves
were cremated
and the salt-sullen water
rose clear.

Thereafter he would say,
The face of God
cannot be described
but I am grateful
I was kneeling.
And the man kneeling
and the man kneeling
heard in his head
a mighty keening.

Who knows what God
in his speaking
said to the man kneeling
but messages lodged in his lungs
were released
as a clean new source of singing.

What else is there
for the eyes to hold in wonder
after they have framed
the face of God?
He spent a lifetime after
alchemizing the visage
from pain and white powder.

Invoke mercy extraordinary
for angels fallen.
Father,
hasten the end.

Jah Music

(For Michael Cooper)

The sound bubbled up
through a cistern one night
and piped its way into
the atmosphere,
and decent people wanted
to know
"What kind of ole nayga music is that
playing on the Government's radio?"
But this red and yellow and dark green
sound,
stained from traveling underground,
smelling of poor people's dinners
from a yard dense as Belgium,
has the healing.
More than weed and white rum healing.
More than bush tea and fever grass cooling
and it pulses without a symphony conductor
all it need is a dub organizer.

Lullaby for Jean Rhys

SLEEP IT OFF LADY
the night nurse is here,
dressed in rain forest colors,
used stars in her hair.
Drink this final dark potion
and straighten your night-dress,
wear your transparent slippers
you must look your best.
For you just might go dancing
atop hard-headed trees
with a man who is virile
and anxious to please.

Sleep now Miss Rhys.

I Am Becoming My Mother

Yellow/brown woman
fingers smelling always of onions   *cook*

My mother raises rare blooms
and waters them with tea   *grow*
her birth waters sang like rivers
my mother is now me

My mother had a linen dress
the color of the sky
and stored lace and damask   *dress*
tablecloths
to pull shame out of her eye.

I am becoming my mother
brown/yellow woman
fingers smelling always of onions.

Guinea Woman

Great grandmother
was a guinea woman
wide eyes turning
the corners of her face
could see behind her,
her cheeks dusted with
a fine rash of jet-bead warts
that itched when the rain set up.

Great grandmother's waistline
the span of a headman's hand,
slender and tall like a cane stalk
with a guinea woman's antelope-quick walk
and when she paused,
her gaze would look to sea
her profile fine like some obverse impression
on a guinea coin from royal memory.

It seems her fate was anchored
in the unfathomable sea
for great grandmother caught the eye of a sailor
whose ship sailed without him from Lucea harbor.
Great grandmother's royal scent of
cinnamon and scallions
drew the sailor up the straits of Africa,
the evidence my blue-eyed grandmother
the first Mulatta,
taken into backra's household
and covered with his name.
They forbade great grandmother's
guinea woman presence.

They washed away her scent of
cinnamon and scallions,
controlled the child's antelope walk,
and called her uprisings rebellions.

But, great grandmother,
I see your features blood dark
appearing
in the children of each new
breeding.
The high yellow brown
is darkening down.
Listen, children,
it's great grandmother's turn.

For Rosa Parks

And how was this soft-voiced woman to know
that this "No"
in answer to the command to rise
would signal the beginning
of the time of walking?
Soft the word
like the closing of some aweful book,
a too-long story
with no pauses for reason,
but yes, an ending
and the signal to begin the walking.
But the people had walked before
in yoked formations down to Calabar,
into the belly of close-ribbed whales,
sealed for seasons
and unloaded to walk again
alongside cane stalks tall as men.
No, walking was not new to them.
Saw a woman tie rags to her feet
running red, burnishing the pavements,
a man with no forty acres
just a mule
riding towards Jerusalem.
And the children small somnambulists
moving in the before-day morning.
And the woman who never raised her voice
never lowered her eyes
just kept walking
leading us towards sunrise.

Bedspread

Sometimes in the still
unchanging afternoons
when the memories crowded
hot and hopeless against
her brow
she would seek its cool colors
and signal him to lie down
in his cell.
It is three in the afternoon Nelson
let us rest here together
upon this bank draped in freedom
color.
It was woven by women with slender
capable hands
accustomed to binding wounds,
hands that closed the eyes of
dead children,
that fought for the right to
speak in their own tongues
in their own land
in their own schools.
They wove the bedspread
and knotted notes of hope
in each strand
and selvaged the edges with
ancient blessings
older than any white man's coming.
So in the afternoons lying on this
bright bank of blessing
Nelson my husband I meet you in dreams
my beloved much of the world too is

asleep blind to the tyranny and evil
devouring our people.
But, Mandela, you are rock on this sand
harder than any metal
mined in the bowels of this land
you are purer than any
gold tempered by fire
shall we lie here wrapped
in the colors of our free Azania?
They arrested the bedspread.
They and their friends are working
to arrest the dreams in our heads
and the women, accustomed to closing
the eyes of the dead
are weaving cloths still brighter
to drape us in glory in a Free
Azania.

Nanny

My womb was sealed
with molten wax
of killer bees
for nothing should enter
nothing should leave
the state of perpetual siege
the condition of the warrior.

From then my whole body would quicken
at the birth of every one of my people's children.
I was schooled in the green-giving ways
of the roots and vines
made accomplice to the healing acts
of Chainey root, fever grass & vervain.

My breasts flattened
settled unmoving against my chest
my movements ran equal
to the rhythms of the forest.

I could sense and sift
the footfall of men
from the animals
and smell danger
death's odor
in the wind's shift.

When my eyes rendered
light from the dark
my battle song opened
into a solitaire's moan

I became most knowing
and forever alone.

And when my training was over
they circled my waist with pumpkin seeds
and dried okra, a traveler's jigida,
and sold me to the traders
all my weapons within me.
I was sent, tell that to history.

When your sorrow obscures the skies
other women like me will rise.

For My Mother (May I Inherit Half Her Stren

My mother loved my father
I write this as an absolute
in this my thirtieth year
the year to discard absolutes

he appeared, her fate disguised,
as a sunday player in a cricket match,
he had ridden from a country
one hundred miles south of hers.

She tells me he dressed the part,
visiting dandy, maroon blazer,
cream serge pants, seam like razor
and the beret and the two-tone shoes.

My father stopped to speak to her sister,
till he looked and saw her by the oleander,
sure in the kingdom of my blue-eyed grandmother.
He never played the cricket match that day.

He wooed her with words and he won her.
He had nothing but words to woo her,
on a visit to distant Kingston he wrote,

"I stood on the corner of King Street and looked,
and not one woman in that town was lovely as you."

My mother was a child of the petite bourgeoisie
studying to be a teacher, she oiled her hands
to hold pens.

My father barely knew his father, his mother died young,
he was a boy who grew with his granny.

My mother's trousseau came by steamer through the snows
    of Montreal
where her sisters Albertha of the cheekbones and the
perennial Rose, combed Jewlit backstreets with French-
turned names for Doris's wedding things.

Such a wedding Harvey River, Hanover, had never seen.
Who anywhere had seen a veil fifteen chantilly yards long?
and a crepe de chine dress with inlets of silk godettes
and a neck-line clasped with jeweled pins!

And on her wedding day she wept. For it was a brazen bride in those days
who smiled.
and her bouquet looked for the world like a sheaf of wheat
against the unknown of her belly,
a sheaf of wheat backed by maidenhair fern, representing Harvey River
her face washed by something other than river water.

My father made one assertive move, he took the imported cherub down
from the heights of the cake and dropped it in the soft territory
between her breasts . . . and she cried.

When I came to know my mother many years later, I knew her as the figure
who sat at the first thing I learned to read: "SINGER," and she breast-fed
my brother while she sewed; and she taught us to read while she sewed and
she sat in judgment over all our disputes as she sewed.

She could work miracles, she would make a garment from a square of cloth
in a span that defied time. Or feed twenty people on a stew made from
fallen-from-the-head cabbage leaves and a carrot and a cho-cho and a palmful
of meat.

And she rose early and sent us clean into the world and she went to bed in
the dark, for my father came in always last.

There is a place somewhere where my mother never took the younger ones
a country where my father with the always smile
my father whom all women loved, who had the perpetual quality of wonder
given only to a child . . . hurt his bride.

Even at his death there was this "Friend" who stood by her side,
but my mother is adamant that that has no place in the memory of
my father.

When he died, she sewed dark dresses for the women amongst us
and she summoned that walk, straight-backed, that she gave to us
and buried him dry-eyed.

Just that morning, weeks after,
she stood delivering bananas from their skin
singing in that flat hill country voice

she fell down a note to the realization that she did
not have to be brave, just this once,
and she cried.

For her hands grown coarse with raising nine children
for her body for twenty years permanently fat
for the time she pawned her machine for my sister's

Senior Cambridge fees
and for the pain she bore with the eyes of a queen

and she cried also because she loved him.

Letters to the Egyptian

1

In case you do not recognize me
when I arrive at Alexandria
I will be wearing a long loose
jade green dress
my hair will be hidden
under a striped fringed headscarf
and I will smell of roseapples and musk.
O love, forgive my vanity,
it is also to make sure
you recognize me
five pounds lighter
drawn from the long journey.
I will bring you a garland
of search-mi-heart leaves
on their underside
I've sewn some woman's tongue seeds.
You said you loved my chatter.

2

When the longboat
drew into Khartoum
where the White Nile meets the Blue
I was tempted to abandon ship.
You see there was this Kushite once
who . . .
But how could he ever
compare to you?
I settled instead for buying
at a bazaar Sheba's silver earrings

facsimiles of tiny steeds they are
sprouting forged feathered wings
for you I found a brass horse
one hand high
you can ride across a table's distance,
some sweet salve for easing knots
in shoulders
and a purchase now private
till we're alone and unveil it.
O how could I have thought of
the Kushite—
And am I now nearer to you?
Does the Nile hold all the world's water?
How far is Khartoum from you?

3

Last night there was such
a storm at sea
I sought level
and chained myself with prayers.
(They held)
and in the after
in the soughing of the wind
I'm sure it was you
I heard sing.
Sleep now beloved
fold yourself in softened sails
I wait for you in the Aftergale.
Calm will be our mooring.

"I Shall Light a Candle of Understanding
in Thine Heart Which Shall Not Be Put Out"
—Esdras

I shall light.
First debts to pay and fences to mend,
lay to rest the wounded past, foes disguised as friends.

I shall light a candle of understanding

Cease the training of impossible hedges round this life
for as fast as you sow them, serendipity's thickets will appear
and outgrow them.

I shall light a candle of understanding in thine heart.

All things in their place then, in this many-chambered heart.
For each thing a place and for HIM a place apart.

I shall light a candle of understanding in thine heart
which shall not be put out.

By the hand that lit the candle.
By the never to be extinguished flame.
By the candle-wax which wind-worried drips
into candle wings luminous and rare.
By the illumination of that candle
exit, death and fear and doubt,
here love and possibility
within a lit heart, shining out.

Songs of Release

I

Free me Rio Negro
for being child of my father
a considerate man
whose motions stirred no stain
to soil your appearances
when he entered you
on Sundays.

Release me O redemption river
waters I have lately seen
for my wanting to sight new Psalms
to wash all hurt hearts clean.

Unbind me now O Blue Nile
for I love your shining son
his hands sailed through my hair
like feluccas heading home.

For I would be boundless
released into space
the creator of all rivers to see.

Free and wash, cleanse unbind
release all rivers, free me.

II

Loose now
the salt cords
binding our tongues

splitting our palettes
causing us to speak blood
curbing the vowels of possibility.
Loose the long-knotted hemp
dragging the old story
the rotted history.
Release grace rains, shower
and water the hope flower.

III

I hold no control, me of myself
I am free
from the considered hold
of frantic fingers
on levers
for when I thought I could hold
HE lifted me, flying free.

Love release, unlock now
must rise above all limits set for me.
I stand with palms open, salute the sun
the old ways over. I newborn one.
I waited for you beautiful teacher
leaning upon the onyx pillar
which supports the wide bridge
over the peril of the river.
You sent a message written in
Amharic on the horizon
I had to read quickly as the sky
was impatient to be going
even reading from this distance
with just opening eyes
was enough for me, the message
spelt "free."

My Last Poem (Again)

I'm approaching the end of my penance of poems.
I can tell because the rosary beads are colder
and it's becoming harder to hold them.

So then, let them go! I'll be glad to see the last of them
once born they sometimes evoked (like most babies)
wonderment. But the delivery of them!
Good-bye poems, you bled me shiny bottles of red feelings.
Poems, you were blood leeches attaching yourself to me
in my should-have-been-brighter moments.
You put to flight lovers who could not compete
you forced yourself into my birthing bed
so I delivered one son and a poem.
When the King of Swords gutted me
and left me for dead, in my insides were found
clots of poems, proving that poets are made of poems
and poems are truth demanding punctuation of light
and your all, and that makes my head vie with night all day.
I don't want to live this way anymore.
Somewhere there is a clean kind man
with a deep and wide understanding
of the mercy and the peace and the infinity.
And we will, if we are lucky, live by the sea
and serve and heal eating of life's salt and bread
and at night lie close to each other and read poems
for which somebody else besides me bled . . .
and that will make me want to write poems.

She Walks into Rooms

She walks into rooms
and they run for towels
say "girl, dry yourself."
And she says no, it's only light
playing upon my water-wave taffeta
dress
But her host put his hand to her face
and it came away wet.
Sometimes at nights
she has to change the sheets,
her favorite brown roses
on a lavender trellis
grow sodden,
and that water has salt
in it
and that's no good for roses.
He left her all this water
to hold in the purple throat
of a flower
it overflowed onto the floors
and her silver shoes sailed
like moon-boats in it.
The water took all the curl
from her hair
it runs slick to her shoulders
where his hands spread
tributaries of rivers.
As he left he said
"It is time to learn to swim."
So saying, he departed to a dry place
carrying silver in his hair

and deep currents in his slightest
motion.
She could have died of cold waiting
in the wet he left there.
But she grew full of mysteries
like the ocean.

Survivor

The strangers passed through here
for years
laying waste the countryside.
They took most living things
even some rare species
with half-extended wings.
They took them all.
Now that genus is extinct.
Lord, they were thorough
in their plunderings.
So, here the wind plays
mourning notes
on bones that once were ribs
(savages) they broke them
when they'd finished eating
and you know how creative
God is with ribs.
That survivor over there
with bare feet and bound hair
has some seeds stored
under her tongue
and one remaining barrel
of rain.
She will go indoors
when her planting is done
loosen her hair
and tend to her son,
and over the bone flute music
and the dead story it tells
listen for grace songs
from her ankle bells.

This Is a Hymn

—For Michael Granzen

For all who ride the trains
all night
sleep on sidewalks and park benches
beneath basements
and abandoned buildings
this is a hymn.

For those whose homes
are the great outdoors
the streets their one big room
for live men asleep in tombs
this is a hymn.

This is a hymn for bag women
pushing rubbish babies
in ridiculous prams
dividing open lots
into elaborate architects' plans.

Mansions of the dispossessed
magnificence of desperate rooms
kings and queens of homelessness
die with empty bottles
rising from their tombs.

This is a hymn
for all recommending
a bootstrap as a way
to rise with effort
on your part.
This is a hymn

may it renew
what passes for your heart.

This hymn
is for the must-be-blessed
the victims of the world
who know salt best
the world tribe
of the dispossessed
outside the halls of plenty
looking in
this is a benediction
this is a hymn.

Dream

An airport waiting room
the decor is perfection
the handiwork of an Eastern lady
skilled in preserving plants
in geometry.
I am seated next to a Western lady
who draws secret pictures
in a book of numbers
and covers her sketches from me.
Then a voice erupts from a
box embedded in the wall
and calls, "All who are from South Africa
must not go forward, must not
board this full freedom-flight
for which we are here waiting."
And a stream of black people exit
driven by the voice in the wall
which uncoils now and is a whip.
A boychild among the driven people
unreels a red kite of a scream
its razor-rigged tail cuts the
bullwhip, a rising red kite of resistance
or a scream lacerates the air
but all the perfect people around
do not hear.
The plane is late
but it will come.
I for one will board,
rise, and if HE wills, sing.
But no matter which heaven
I ascend to or whose hymns of praise

I bring, that scream
will be a red girdle around my belly
from a child who could have been born
from me,
a child whose tongue is surer
around the name Azania.
To all the perfect people—Azania
who wait in this terminal—Azania
know that this scream will grow—Azania
to strangle your dreams—Azania
for no one is free—Azania
till the people of Azania
are free to board this plane.
Azania, O people
O kites of freedom
Azania in our childrens' names.

Gleanings

Often, it's a field at dark
where the hooded bowed outcasts
go after the reapers have passed
collecting then the gleanings.

Sometimes after the harvest is in
and the fields are lying spent
they still move in twilight foraging
for the seeds the birds have missed.

(What a hard time the post-harvest is!)

We glean outside the system
our candidate did not win.
We glean outside our father's yard
the stewards are self-serving.

We glean outside the temples of fullness
for charity dropped careless
from full sheaves above.
It is time to come into the kingdom.

Some Nights I Don't Sleep

Some nights, I don't sleep
for having in my possession
aweful chips of information
lodged in my memory
separating me from rest.

Like I read once
in a woman's magazine
a description by an impressed woman
of the color, depth, and size
of a South American general's
bedroom eyes.

And maybe she did not know
about bodies floating
in the water system
and shocking stadiums
running with young blood
and live men
cemented into silence
and the eruption within
the heart of the high poet
of Machu Picchu.

I don't sleep some nights
because I once saw a photograph
of my son's double.
He lives in Soweto.
They both have eyes ancient
long as the Nile

eyes that are witness
to every fall every rise
of our people's fortunes
and I don't sleep good
when I think of them/him.

Some nights are divided
four ways
quartered and a moon.

First quarter
a meditation to lift
the legacy of stone
some would will
to the wild children
who call this city's streets home.

The next quarter
a sankey to bide-up
the broken of the dispossessed
who are now eating garbage
that trickled down
from what's left.

The third quarter
is a join-up
a mantra
to contain
the false consciousness
the teachings in the church
of every man for himself.
A mantra to transcend
their twisted anthem

"What's love got to do with it."

Sing, O children of light, sing
For love is all and everything.

For in the fourth quarter
in the promised light
before dawn
the cycle
the spiral
will have gone
full circle
and
we will meet ourselves
at the starting-over side
to bury this bitterness
with green bush
never to rise.

So, allow then
the undivided healing trees
to make black pepper grains
blow easy in the doctor breeze.
Before this thing is done
we will know real sleep.
Light filled and lulled
by a more merciful breeze.
So to wake now don't really matter
for some night is not for sleep
is to use collective light
as laser beams
to clear the home stretch
to Heartease.

Upon a Quarter Million

Upon a quarter million
With a tape deck of gold
O measure me a mile
of sweet vintage Bob Andy.
Rocking steady
on a pointed principle
Alton Ellis is showing me why
Because he is "Just a guy."
And when I feel it too sweet now
I can't take it no more
The Cables make a connection
from the sky, and ask me "Why,
baby tell me why?"
Sitting beside me
upon this song sentimental journey
is a man with the name "Levi"
written across the front of him creppe.
And I surmise, it must be the name
of his tribe.
And then I think, No, it must be
his rightful name.
For sometimes it would suit a one
to write him name upon himself.
In case Babylon stop you
and fraid claim your tongue
in which case you could just
look down and remind you eye
and say "Yes oppressor
I name is Levi."

Upon a quarter million
with a tape deck of gold
the driver cut a corner
on the bias
and pitch up by the park.
And it come to me
that I must praise all of life
when it light and when it dark.
For all of it is life
and life is all of that
and as I think this so,
I just reach my stop.

Some of My Worst Wounds

Some of my worst wounds
have healed into poems.
A few well-placed
stabs in the back
have released a singing
trapped between my shoulders.
A carrydown
has lent leverage
to the tongue's rise
and betrayals sent words
hurrying home
to toe the line again.

In Anxiety Valley

Down here again
can't see a thing except dark.
Now sometimes dark is pleasing
like on a tall slim one
or on a dress you wear
with wine-colored underthings.

This dark though
is the fallout from the shadow
and the fear combined, exploding.
God has got me on hold
and the receptionist
keeps insisting
"He's not in."
And so I have to be here waiting
down here with the rest of the heathen.
I keep insisting
"I must talk to him,
my complaint can't bear waiting."
And she shouts "wait."
So I'm down here
where the dark matches my hair
and so they will mistake me
for a bald head
and make me wait
and make me wait.

I have to get out of here.
I have to get out of here
before the next plague comes

the plague and other things
which I have been imagining.
(That's really what I wanted
to talk to God about,
my terrible imaginings.)
I'll try a constant pleading
make my fingertips flutter
a nervous kete . . . a hint
to Him . . .
or keep really silent
till an answer comes.
God speaks in silence,
or responds to drums.

Heartease I

We with the straight eyes
and no talent for cartography
always asking
"How far is it to Heartease?"
and they say,
"Just around the corner."

But that being the spider's direction
means each day finds us further away.
Dem stick wi up
dem jook wi down
and when dem no find
what dem come fi find
them blood we and say
"walk wid more next time."

So, take up divining again
and go inna interpretation
and believe the flat truth
left to dry on our tongues.
Truth say,
Heartease distance
cannot hold in a measure
it say
travel light
you are the treasure.
It say
you can read map
even if you born
a Jubilee
and grow with your granny

and eat crackers for your tea.
It say
you can get license
to navigate
from sail board horse
in the sea's gully.

Believe, believe
and believe this
the eye know how far
Heartease is.

Heartease II

In what looked like the blackout last week
a meteorite burst from the breast of the sky
smoking like a censer, it spelled out in
incandescent calligraphy
a message for all who had deep eyes.

If you did not see it I'll tell you what
it said:
Cultivate the search-mi-heart and
acres of sincerity grass and turn your
face towards Heartease.

Set out a wash pan and catch mercy rain
forget bout drought, catch the mercy rain,
bathe and catch a light from this meteoric flame
and sit down cleansed, to tell a rosary of your
ancestor's names,
a singing chain of ancient names to bind them tight
all who work evil downward through the night.

    And toward morning the sun come and tell you
    "sleep, I'll mark your place with this azure/rose ribbon
    taken from the hidden locks of the dawn
    sleep in the day and you will dream when you sleep
    the second surah of this message."

And who hear, do all that and sleep in the darkened day and
dream as them sleep, how the one whose hand draw the veil,
(for it was not a blackout) the one who fling the meteor
was in a celestial vexation
saying, Imagine, how I put you here so in this most favored place

and look how you take it and less count it.
Look how you root up my rarest blooms,
look how you take my flower bed dem turn tombs,
look how you eye red from looking over a next one yard
from envying everything him have.
Like him concrete-stressed-cast-iron-lawn
and him man-made-robot-made-by-man-to-replace-man,
you want to know how far this thing gone?
Some calling Siberia a nice open land.
At this point it look like him was too grieved to go on
him had to drink some dew water from the throat
of a glass-petaled flower.
And when his wrath was dampened he spoke again:

I have many names and one is merciful . . .
So in that name I have decided that the veil I draw
will be lifted, when you look to the condition of
your part of this yard.
When you stop draw blood cross the promise line in the
young people's palms.
When the scribes cleanse their hands and rise to write
new psalms.
When you sight up why outta the whole human race
is you of all people I choose to dwell in this place.
So who hear send me here to tell you say
we do not know bout the intentions of a next one
but we catching mercy rain in zinc and tub pan
and in addition
to the search-mi-heart
the sincerity seeds
and the pilgrimage to Heartease
we planting some one-love
undivided ever-living healing trees
and next week if you want to come, welcome
for we going to set up again
to extend the singing rosary of our ancestors' names
till the veil is rent from the eyes of the sky

of everyone
forever and ever
illumination.

Heartease III

In this year of cataclysm pre-predicted
being plagued with dreams
of barefoot men marching
and tall civilizations crumbling
forward to where the gathering, gathering.
Crowdapeople, crowdapeople weep and mourn,
crowdapeople I have seen
packed in Japanese carriers
dark corpses of fallen warriors.
A man wearing a dub image of dirt
roots for fodder in a garbage can
raises a filth-encrusted hand
in a dumb acceptance/greeting
of the stasis on the land.
You see it crowdapeople?

Look and marvel
for I have seen the wonder
of the candyman's posse
women laden like caravels with gold
trimmed in fur, booted in leather
crowned in picture hats
skeeled O Panama.

higgler
women who
buy goods
cheap &
sell them
(unedu. working
class trades)

O wear all this together
in the height of 98-degree weather.
Be acquainted with things to come,
behold the force transparent
mirror the cynical face of the crowd.
Lead them down to dungeons of slackness
everybody follow.

Soak them in the river of darkness
everybody wallow.

Crowdapeople, crowdapeople.
Big Massa knows
that them powder the devil
and sell you
fi draw him up yu nose.
Crowdapeople,
settle.
Crowdapeople,
level.
When you gone so wide
you will encounter
your true selves again
from the starting-over side.

Then . . .
Say of the waters of the Hope river
how much sweeter than the ferment wine,
say of the simple leavened loaf
"you are the wafer."
Accept this healing unbeliever
place truth on your tongue deceiver.
Gather, for the days wrongly predicted
by short-tongued ones will end,
these days are but a confused overture to the real
movement, to the pulsing of the rhythms of the
first and last grouping,
we will rise triumphant, clean singing.
For the righteous planted in this place,
have access unlimited to the gardens of grace.
I speak no judgment
this voice is to heal
to speak of possibility
for in dreams Big Massa show me
say,

mercantilism = evil

"I know my people, I created them
their ways are strange only to who will
not love and accept them,
what they do best is to be."
No judgment I speak
that function is not mine
I come only to apply words
to a sore and confused time.

So . . .
If we mix a solution
from some wild bees' honey
and some search-mi-heart extract
better than red conscience money
and we boil it in a bun-pan
over a sweet wood fire
make the soft smell of healing
melt hard hearts and bare wire.
If we take it and share it
so everyone get a taste
and it reach till
it purge evil from this place
till we start again clean
from the birthplace
of the stream,
while above us arches
the mercy span
a high onyx beam;
reaching from the sea
to the cobalt
blue mountain ridge
the azure forgiving
of the wide mercy bridge.

And . . .
Suppose we call out the
singers and musicians

by their hidden holy names
and then pull out from the belly
bottom of the drum and the bass
chords that quake evil and
make holy spirit raise,
while the rest of we planting the
undivided, ever-living
healing trees,
what a glory
possibility
soon come
HEARTEASE . . .

Heartease New England 1987

I see a bird trapped
under the iron girders of the Ashmont station overpass.
It is trying to measure the distance between columns
with its given wing span, and it fails
for being alone and not having a wing span wide enough.
I am told that birds travel faster over greater distances
when they move in chevron formation
a group of birds could measure the width of the Ashmont
station overpass . . . I know how the bird feels.
I have come to see the backyards of the richest lands
on earth, their basements, their backrooms,
I have seen the poor asleep in carcasses of rooms.
Those who sleep together are fortunate
not to be one of the ultimate dispossessed
the truly homeless are usually alone
and tend to wakefulness.
In the fall I search for signs
a pattern in the New England flaming trees
"What is my mission? Speak, leaves"
(for all journeys have hidden missions).
The trees before dying, only flame brighter
maybe that is the answer, live glowing while you can.

That is the only answer, except one evening in November
I see an African in Harvard Square.
He is telling himself a story as he walks
in telling it, he takes all the parts
and I see that he has taken himself home.
And I have stories too, until I tell them
I will not find release, that is my mission.
Some nights though, anxiety assails me

a shroud spinning in the snow.
They say it's the affliction of this age,
it appears unasked, an unwelcome companion
who always wants you
to sit down and die with him
when for your own good you should keep going.
I know how the bird trying to measure the overpass
feels.
I too can never quite get the measure of this world's structure
somewhere I belong to community, there
I am part of a grouping of many souls and galaxies
I am part of something ever evolving, familiar, and most mighty.
I reaffirm this knowing one evening, a Wednesday
as I go up Shephard Street. Someone is playing
Bob Marley and the notes are levitating
across the Garden Street end of the street.
They appear first as notes and then feather into birds
pointing their wings, arranging themselves for traveling
long distances.
And birds are the soul's symbol, so I see
that I am only a sojourner here but I came as friend
came to record and sing and then, depart.
For my mission this last life is certainly this
to be the sojourner poet caroling for peace
calling lost souls to the way of Heartease.

Come Let Your Eyes Feel

Come let your eyes feel
the colors, the landscape
of Heartease
the long day will pass
drawn lightly through rays
of African Star grass
and at night a bed-tranquil
borrowed from rest
and pillows all peaceful
an heart's ease is this.

Star Suite

i

Asi itra, star
is come
and hangs low
over Blue Mountain.

Asi itra woman star
beams in
pleased with being.
See the silver points
of her light chain mail
skirts and the moonstone
anchoring her waist
and I say, "such splendor"
(with some envy)
for being only a woman
hovering between earth
and star reality.

ii

Asi itra is not sure
I deserve to have
close contact with her
because she is star
and I'm only me.

But this lady
who is in charge
of all women
told her

"go to her (me)
remind her I'm who
gave her the flower."
The flower!
Let me tell you,
there is no name for its
species.
No wine/peach pomegranate
bloom
extended on a celadon green
stem
anywhere near it
has ever been seen.
But she plucked it
from the bower of start-over
in the garden of visions
like a slender-fingered
conjurer
and gave it to me as my own.
And if she sent you
then you'd better come too
star skirted
moonstone belted
silver striped tresses,
Miss Beauty Queen of all stars
Sister, Asi itra.

Star Suite II

Faith star i

Though clouds veil your shining
you are there
behind ripped sheets of storm
confusion you are there
and manifest brilliant
even more so
when the lower world
spins in darkness.

Starfish ii

Your earth facsimile is a crustacean
and being of the earth, don't glow
but takes low in the sand
scrubbing the sea's floor
and pretends to like living so.
O starfish fallen
dried out, you harden
and in hardening
opalescent you glow.

Rainstar iii

I saw you once
pinned onto a cloud cushion
and another poet said
that it couldn't be true,
stars don't shine from the center
of clouds,
but he didn't know
you, bright star triumphant.
Rain star regenerating
morning star promised at
birth
swan star transfigured
moon star mystic
phoenix star
rising
from the many ends of the earth.
Wear her light around you
peace within
about you
grace and joy now follow
rise O rise O star.

The Pictures of My New Day

The pictures of my new day
will now be colored, drawn,
by the tempera of first light
stored for me by a thoughtful dawn
who knew of my love for late sleeping.

Now, more than love on earth,
the untamed imaginings rooted under
my hair,
more than the sanded varnished scars
jeweled now I wear,
more than the silver life sign of survival
and the paid penance of poems,
this light.
It flared up one evening, a Sunday
towards seven.
I swear it descended a living shaft
of brightest light
lit from within by light.
And as if sighting the woman's love
of show
not content with the perfection of itself
perfect pole running floor to ceiling
to floor
it spawned and spiraled from itself
ribbons and banners of light, more light.
I have seen it.

O Love You So Fear the Dark

O love, you so fear the dark
you so accustomed to fighting.
It only seems like the night
but it's a veiled overture to light.
It is transitory love, it is passing.
The dagger, love, sheath it.
The bloodied dove, sweet, release it.
There is nothing to fear
it is dark only as your eyes
or my hair
and it is kind love
it leads to light
if you but knew it
only unarmed will you go through it.

Farewell Wild Woman (I)

I seemed to have put distance
between me and the wild woman
she being certified bad company.
Always inviting me to drink
bloody wine from clay cups
and succumb to false promise
in the yes of slim dark men.
Sometimes though when I'm
closing the house down early
and feeling virtuous for living
one more day without falling too low
I think I see her behind the hibiscus
in dresses competing with their red,
and she's spinning a key hung on a
cat's-eye ring
and inviting me to go low riding.

Farewell Wild Woman (II)

Sometime in this first half
the wild woman left.
Rumor spreads a story
that bad love killed her
kinder ones swear
that just like that,
she dreamed herself
off precipices
sheer as her dresses.

Only I think I know
where she went,
(I might even have hidden her
myself)
in a priest's hole
at the side of this house
and feed her occasionally
with unscorched bits of memory.

Ceremony for the Banishment of
the King of Swords

I know, you woke up with the fever rising like sulphur
from the wounds
And the pain which sank you to sleep has pierced you
awake this morning
On top of which you have at work, your own cat-o-nine
beating yourself
Because you did it again, aligned yourself to such a source
of treachery and pain
And his calling card is lying careless on your pillow,
behold the King of Swords, upon his entrance cauterizing
fire follows
The King of Swords lives within Tarot, to all appearances
he is the shining one
Countenance like a promise and a forehand rising lily-like
from a stem
and that hand bids you "come just come," and you go
(from within knowledge I know)

Go, and just when you get close enough to the seeming
"here is rest"
Firm, broad, sure expanse that is his chest, quick as you can
say "heart"
He unsheathes the sword aligned with his backbone and sinks it
into your chest.
I must leave you lying with the no-mercy of steel piercing you
But you have to hold it till it's all released, this final wounding
is for your healing.

The King of Swords is a master of disguise (sometimes he is a woman)
Whatever skin he is traveling in there is one condition
for his coming.
Le Roi requires weakness. Or maybe an excess of feeling
like you're strong, over a not so sure foundation . . .
and here he comes, setting himself up as solid ground
watch for the inclining lily of the forehand bidding you "come."
Admit it, something, a persistent singing under your singing
was warning you
A counter-melody crooning "careful" under what became your song
"this-time-da-da-what-I've-been-waiting-for."
And beneath an indigo layer of notes intoned careful warning
but you were not listening.
Ahh, if only you had heard with your soul, if your eyes had not
been taken in
By the vast varied sideshow of his tricks . . . hey! red feathers
falling, voodoo sleight of hand, juggling words of together
forever, alizarian helium balloons of promises and a rush
of fallen-from-paradise birds rising like riots from his hat.
But the real feature is the sword, the heart of the killer act.
Sometimes when he smiles you see the metallic lining of his lips
and you think it's the gleam in your eyes, besides the song is up
on full now "I want you because I need you so."
In all honesty the King says he does not want to wound.
But most times he says he is perfect and you're the one with
the problem
because you won't sit still on a Sunday afternoon
when you want to rest within a color like aquamarine
and just be and he wants to practise stabbings.
Get up now if you can, here will enter a wise woman.

Wise woman: "Remove it from the personal, that is the first thing
    and know you have been elected for all of us to go through
    this and go through this again, so you can penetrate it,
    write it down, so more of us can recognize it,

so more of us don't have to choose him . . . don't weep,
so more us can be vulnerable in peace.

But you really don't want to hear this, you are screaming how it hurts
so
Between the last and floating rib, in the belly where the spirit lives,
behind the eyes at the corners of the smile and yes, it hurts everywhere
doesn't it?
But hear this, it will be a worse hurt everytime until you recognize
him.
Do you think you can now? do you know his name? then identify him!
Uncover him! Shame him! show his face like they do to stubborn corpses
who resist final burial.
Uncover him, shame him and yours, ours will be the victory.
You will never see him again. In his place will come . . . What do you want?
a prince . . . or personal peace? this last reward is better than all others.
Remove his ring, do not honor him. He rules over the people
and the state of whole countries is a testimony to his warlike wounding.
Next, admit the shame. Because everyone is walking around with bright-
colored garments hiding their sores and expensive veilings
shading their hurting.
So they elected you, wounded one, to end this thing.
To uncover and lay open this nine-night living-dead thing.
An end to this always making bad choices . . . sing
"This is the ending, this is the beginning."

If you have a lovely light that you are carrying
and it caught from what would seem like nothing.
Maybe some good foreparents did
or a holy and felicitous sparking
like one day, you were standing under
a benevolent section of the sky
and a little wisp of ether flew low
and brushed over the need for a light
in your heart.
And the needs ignited and a grace-light
started

And you were so careful carrying it
from the beginning
Fanning it with prayers and clean
living
and it grew bright enough for others
to see it
and some days you found you could warm
someone else with it
or someone saw it and wanted a light
of their own
so they smile and a smile is a start
for a light of your own.
There is, though, this warning.
When you feel that your light is so bright
there is no need to tend it
when you feel that your light
is so strong
you forget where it came from
enter the king
and you know about the sword
and you know about the wounding.
You can get up now
leave the tomb empty
leave the broken sword there
here is the chant of light
the new source of singing
this is the ending
this is the beginning.

THE CHANT OF LIGHT

We have light.
Only who gave it
can put it out.
We have light
diffusing dark
canceling doubt,

even when the point
of the poisoned sword
injects venom and dark
a light running
like mercury
through the veins
is a shining antidote
to pain.
King of Swords
You are no more
We have light
You see
We have light.

Blue Peace Incantation

Within blue of peace,
the azure of calm,
beat soft now, bright heart,
beat soft, sound calm.
By cobalt of love deep
indigo of perception
by waters of sky blue
by need's incantation
be measured
blue measured
in verdant balance
of green
heart be rocked calm now
light we have seen.
By meditations of
clear waters,
all strivings cease,
within all,
illumination,
forever, lasting blue peace.

And You Being So Abundantly
Blessed with Names

And you being so abundantly blessed with names
I strive to commit each one to memory
to each is attached a glimpse of your face
to each a revelation a key to your infinity.
A recitation of your names is a singing
shining chain binding us to you
round perfect as the moon's face
we stand in the circle of light that is you.
The everlasting luminous go-round of your names
we chant them, order them to lists
arrange them in a disc, color them differently
our favorites.
But they are all our favorites.
We love your names and yet
the life task of wordsmiths must now be,
from the fire of the soul's refining
to forge more names for your shining
for the sum of the names we know now
is not equal to
the smallest glory that is you.

A Rosary of Your Names

God your face made manifest
on surfaces of sand or water.
In the spring balance of the green
your face is everything.
Dark in learning
revelation into light
your face is day
your face is night.
In topaz and rubies
in small sea stones
in the warmth of flesh yearnings
in the armature of bones.
Everywhere
in chiaroscuro
now dark
now light
in the balance of green
in the light
in the light.
In the rose soul's unfolding
sing
God dawns as morning.
Lord of trains
and things flying.
Creator of ether, land,
and oceans,
let truth now stand.
Your names are infinity
light and possibility
and right
and blessed

and upfull
and most of all merciful
and song
to you we belong.
And the last and the hidden
and the wonderful
and in the name of what was dead
and now lives, awaken
again song, resurrection.
And behold the bridegroom cometh
and his sighs are the sound of flutes
and the benediction
is the rain falling from your hands.
And release, release now
an end to pain
within the stillness of surrender
all striving cease
in the telling of your names rosary
peace be, Heartease.

A Rosary of Your Names (II)

The Merciful
The Peace
The Source
The Hidden
The All Strivings Cease.
The One
The First
The Bridge
The Last
The Height
The Ocean
The Promise come to pass
The Blessing
The Beloved
most Beloved
In whose eyes worlds live
The Everlasting
The First Song
The Maker of Mountains
The Give
The Most Blessed
The Belong
The Architect of Planets
The One in Charge
Superior
Almighty
All Knowing
Large
There is no God But God
Who lit the First Flame
Orchestrator of Dawns and Sunsets

chant a rosary of Your Names
Painter of limitless palette
Harpmaker, song giver
Light which takes wings
God is
God is
Infinity
Blessings.

Always Homing Now Soul Toward Light

Always homing now soul toward light,
want like wings beating
against the hold-back of dark.

Above the face of yet another city
bright with bright points of seduction
I hover, and know from having been there
that the lights of cities go under,
their brilliance is not what
this soul is after.
Night swallows the sunset now
the lips of the horizon come together
and there is in all this dark sky
only one thin line of glow.
When the lips close finally
it will seem (be warned)
it will seem like the dark has won.
But is only the interim
before the true shining comes.
Light is close sometimes,
it seems to burnish my limbs
some nights.
And for wanting it so
I'm a child then
who must sleep with some
small part of light
from a connection above
my head.
Surround us while we sleep, light
encircling
light in rings marrying me to

source.
To me, I say, fold the dark dresses
of your youth
let the silver run like comets'
tails through your hair.
For me, I know, the light in me
does not want to be hidden anymore,
anywhere.

The Woman Speaks to the Man
Who Has Employed Her Son

Her son was first made known to her
as a sense of unease, a need to cry
for little reasons and a metallic tide
rising in her mouth each morning.
Such signs made her know
that she was not alone in her body.
She carried him full term
tight up under her heart.

She carried him like the poor
carry hope, hope you get a break
or a visa, hope one child go through
and remember you. He had no father.
The man she made him with had more
like him, he was fair-minded
he treated all his children
with equal and unbiased indifference.

She raised him twice, once as mother
then as father, set no ceiling
on what he could be doctor,
earth healer, pilot take wings.
But now he tells her he is working
for you, that you value him so much
you give him one whole submachine gun
for him alone.

He says you are like a father to him
she is wondering what kind of father

would give a son hot and exploding
death, when he asks him for bread.
She went downtown and bought three
and one-third yards of black cloth
and a deep crowned and veiled hat
for the day he draws his bloody salary.

She has no power over you and this
at the level of earth, what she has
are prayers and a mother's tears
and at knee city she uses them.
She says psalms for him
she reads psalms for you
she weeps for his soul
her eyewater covers you.

She is throwing a partner
with Judas Iscariot's mother
the thief on the left-hand side
of the cross, his mother
is the banker, her draw though
is first and last for she still
throwing two hands as mother and father.
She is prepared, she is done. Absalom.

Recommendation for Amber

With her, you would have a guide
to the small nubians in the garden.
They live only under bushes
that have never known knives.

They come out at night
riding on seasonal cicadas
whose noise is a radar guide,
they have given her minute boxes

of see-in eye ointment.
A very little rubbed on the eyes
makes you see good duppies.
With her Mondays could be Sundays

She would go to church on Monday
then stay indoors all afternoon
sleeping, because there is no
difference in days with Amber.

No matter how she tries she loses
things (she is not orderly).
But she will summon them back again
by invoking their names over and over.

So if you pass outside her window
and hear her repeating insistently
"keys" or "comb," just know
that this is her strange ceremony,

the finding of lost objects.
Invariably she finds what's missing
or if it's taken, in its place will come
something amazingly much better.

She is blessed with a remarkable nose,
she can identify the ingredients
in perfumes just so, like she can
isolate the trail of the gentle tuberose

from beneath the more sensual oil slick
smell of the cat glands secreting civet.
She also knows the secret properties
of gemstones. Take amber itself, her name.

Though neither rare, costly, nor a gem
but the golden night sweat of a tree
compassionate and resilient, it's special
because it is self-healing.

Despite her tendency to wearing her hair
wild and her slow Egyptian eyes which are
fixed always above her employer's head
she has a good hand at plain cooking.

On Becoming a Tiger

The day that they stole her tiger's-eye ring
was the day that she became a tiger.
She was inspired by advice received from Rilke

who recommended that, if the business of drinking
should become too bitter,
that one should change oneself into wine.

The tiger was actually always asleep
inside her, she had seen it
stretched out, drowsing and inert

when she lay upon her side and stared
for seven consecutive days into a tall mirror
that she had turned on its side.

Her focus had penetrated all exterior
till at last she could see within her
a red glowing landscape of memory and poems,

a heart within her heart
and lying there big, bright, and golden
was the tiger, wildly darkly striped.

At night she dreams that her mother
undresses her and discovers that, under
her outerwear, her bare limbs are marked

with the broad and urgent striations
of the huge and fierce cat of Asia
with the stunning golden quartz eyes.

She has taken to wearing long dresses
to cover the rounded tail coiling behind her.
She has filled her vases with tiger lilies

and replaced her domestic cat
with a smaller relative of hers, the ocelot.
At four in the morning she practices stalking

up and down the long expanse of the hall.
What are the ingredients in tiger's milk?
Do tigers ever mate for life?

Can she rewrite the story of Little Black Sambo?
Can a non-tiger take a tiger for a wife?
To these and other questions,

she is seeking urgent answers
now that she is living an openly
tigerly life.

Love Song of Cane in Three Parts

One day in the field I just look up and see him watching me.
I look up at the same time that him pause
machete riveted against the sky. Flat silver scimitar
against the sky.
All around us were pointed lances of green, our feelings
the only things of tenderness in that place.
We stayed there a long time, so still, recognizing
each other, till the stretched-out moment snapped us
back to this place.
He brought the machete down to his side.
He said afterwards that he could never cut anything
when I look like that at him.
I asked him if he wanted water, he said "yes," but after
he said that he was thinking that it was life that I
would give to him.

I know the exact moment that I saw her. It was the same moment
that I loved her.
It just became a fact, a true word in that same instant.
If I was a man who wear a watch I could have matched that knowing
to an exact number, but this was witnessed by the sun.
And in telling you now, I can say it was during the second
half of the day that I saw her.
And the moment that I did, the sun suddenly ceased to beat down
so unmerciful
but slipped over into the time of cool, the easier time
of afternoon.

Something happens when we love. In some ways it is outside telling.
Lying face to face we utter groanings that cannot be explained
and talk in tongues, glossolalia, we sing in the language

of our tribe.

When his hand presses the base of my throat, my voice box
springs open and releases a rush of vocal memories,

of the times we ran naked together as children by the river
and caught small fish

and waved at our water selves waving back to us from the river's
surface.

It is then, released by memory, sure of our twinship, that our duet
swells high and escalating

and in a language known to no outsiders, indivisible, we sing.

Mother the Great Stones Got to Move

Mother, one stone is wedged across the hole in our history
and sealed with blood wax.
In this hole is our side of the story, exact figures,
headcounts, burial artifacts, documents, lists, maps
showing our way up through the stars; lockets of brass
containing all textures of hair clippings.
It is the half that has never been told, some of us
must tell it.

Mother, there is the stone on the hearts of some women and men
something like an onyx, cabochon-cut
which hung on the wearer seeds bad dreams. Speaking for the small
dreamers of this earth, plagued with nightmares, yearning
for healing dreams
we want that stone to move.

Upon an evening like this, mother, when one year is making way
for another, in a ceremony attended by a show of silver stars,
mothers see the moon, milk-fed, herself a nursing mother
and we think of our children and the stones upon their future
and we want these stones to move.

For the year going out came in fat at first
but towards the harvest it grew lean.
And many mouth corners gathered white
and another kind of poison, powdered white
was brought in to replace what was green.
And death sells it with one hand
and with the other death palms a gun
then death gets death's picture
in the papers asking,

"where does all this death come from?"
Mother, stones are pillows
for the homeless sleep on concrete sheets.
Stone flavors soap, stone is now meat,
the hard-hearted giving our children
stones to eat.

Mother, the great stones over mankind got to move.
It's been ten thousand years we've been watching them now
from various points in the universe.
From the time of our birth as points of light
in the eternal coiled workings of the cosmos.
Roll away stone of poisoned powders come
to blot out the hope of our young.
Move stone of sacrificial lives we breed
to feed to tribalistic economic machines.
From across the pathway to mount morning
site of the rose quartz fountain
brimming anise and star water
bright fragrant for our children's future.
Mother these great stones got to move.

White Birds

At first, we liked to describe them
as doves,
the white pigeons who came to live
at this house.
Appearing first as a circle with wings,
then some blessing pulling the circle in,
so that its center became our house.
Now in these eaves
a benediction of bird.
Their nervous hearts
in sync enough
with our rhythms
they enter into this house.
So sometimes in the middle
of doing some woman's thing
I look up to find us
in a new painting.
House in a rock
with wooden floors
a boy and white pigeons.